EGYPT'S NEW REGIME AND THE FUTURE OF THE U.S.-EGYPTIAN STRATEGIC RELATIONSHIP

The revolution in Egypt in January-February 2011 that removed President Hosni Mubarak from power has resulted in profound changes to the Egyptian domestic scene. Authority has passed from a long-standing authoritarian president to a military government and has now entered a phase in which a new president, originally from the once-banned Muslim Brotherhood, is trying to exercise real power not only over the civilian government, but over the military establishment as well. Meanwhile, an activist judiciary has disbanded the original body charged to write Egypt's new constitution as well as the parliament that was elected in late 2011-early 2012 that came to be dominated by the Brotherhood. As of this writing, Egypt still must pass through several more political hurdles—the drafting of a new constitution by a newly-constituted body selected for that task, passage of this constitution by way of a public referendum, and new parliamentary elections—before we know what type of political system will emerge in the country and the main political forces that will shape its future.

For the time being, Egypt's powerful military establishment has acquiesced to the new president's decision to shake up the military hierarchy.[1] In August 2012, President Mohammed Morsi retired Defense Minister, Field Marshal Hussein Tantawi, head of the Supreme Council of the Armed Forces (SCAF), and his deputy in the SCAF, army chief of staff General Sami Anan, as well as the chiefs of the navy, air force, and air defense commands. He had previously retired the head of Egypt's intelligence service. He has replaced these figures with a younger generation of military men.[2] Although Morsi took a political gamble against the old guard within the SCAF and won, it is still unclear how far his authority reaches. Significantly, Morsi did not choose a civilian to head the Defense Ministry, but instead chose an officer who was head of military intelligence and a member of the SCAF to be Tantawi's replacement. Although rumors abound in Cairo that Morsi wants to exercise full civilian control over the military (including over its nontransparent budget), he was careful not to go too far. The military still retains control over its vast economic enterprises, which some analysts suggest may represent as much as 20-25 percent of the country's gross domestic product (GDP).[3]

Amid these political changes is the growing insecurity in the Sinai region bordering Israel and the Gaza Strip. The Sinai, long neglected by Cairo except for the popular tourist destinations in the south, has become a sort of Wild West. Northern Sinai is populated by a combustible mix of disaffected Bedouin tribes, jihadists from outside of Egypt, some radical Palestinian extremists from Gaza, and home-grown Egyptian terrorists, many of whom were released from prison during the revolution in early 2011. In early August 2012, a group of extremists killed 16 Egyptian soldiers guarding the border region in an operation that was aimed at striking Israel, prompting the Egyptian military to take retaliatory strikes in the area and destroying many of the tunnels that have been used by the extremists to smuggle goods and weapons from Sinai into the Gaza Strip and vice-versa.[4] More such incidents are likely in the future.

Key questions for U.S. foreign policy and defense officials are: How does the United States maintain good relations and preserve its strategic partnership with Egypt under its new political leadership and a changing political environment? How does the United States do so while it adheres to American values such as supporting a democratic transition even when democratic processes may result in political actors coming to power who do not share U.S. foreign policy and security goals?

EGYPT'S IMPORTANCE TO U.S. STRATEGIC GOALS IN THE REGION

A cursory glance at a map of the Middle East shows how pivotal Egypt is to U.S. strategic goals. It is on the same latitude as the Persian Gulf through which a significant share of the world's oil still passes (making overflight and refueling stops in Egypt for U.S. military aircraft headed to that region all the more important, especially during times of crisis), and its Suez Canal is a key transit waterway for U.S. naval ships passing from the Mediterranean to the Red Sea and then on to the Arabian Sea and the Persian Gulf. In a report released publicly in 2006, the U.S. Government Accountability Office noted that between 2001 and 2005, the Egyptian government provided overflight permission to 36,553 U.S. military aircraft and granted expedited transit of 861 U.S. naval ships through the Suez Canal.[5] Such figures underscore the importance of Egypt for U.S. strategic planners. In addition, Egypt borders Israel and the Gaza Strip, making it an important player, strategically and politically, in the Israeli-Palestinian situation. Egypt also borders Libya to its west and Sudan to its south, both countries that can impact its security.

As the most populous country in the Arab world (estimates are that its population may now be about 85 million), and one that houses important intellectual centers—such as Al-Azhar University, the leading institute of religious education in the Sunni Muslim world, and longstanding secular institutions like Cairo University—and has been a leader in the region in terms of the development of political parties and civic organizations (Egypt's Bar Association, for example, was started in 1912)—what happens in Egypt is closely watched by people and governments throughout the region. Moreover, Egypt has long considered itself a leader of the Arab world, even when other countries have eclipsed this role.[6]

Since the 1970s, when the late Egyptian President Anwar Sadat switched sides in the Cold War, Egypt has been considered an important strategic asset for the United States. The U.S.-brokered Camp David Accords in 1978 and the Egyptian-Israeli peace treaty in 1979 brought Egypt closer into the U.S. camp. Although Egypt entered into these arrangements for its own national security interests, its positions conformed to U.S. strategic goals at the time of keeping Egypt outside of the Soviet orbit and lessening the chances of another major Arab-Israeli war.[7] Since that time, Egypt has been a major recipient of U.S. financial assistance, receiving about $1.3 billion in military aid annually, which has held steady for more than 30 years, as well as substantial civilian aid (which was $800 million for many years and is now between $200 million and $300 million a year).

This aid, particularly the military assistance, has been seen as an important barometer of U.S. support for Egypt and has weathered several stormy patches in the relationship. But this aid has also been problematic on a political level. Many political figures in the United States consider the aid to be a form of leverage over Egypt and believe it entitles the United States to expect certain norms of behavior from the Egyptian government. From the Egyptian perspective, the aid is the least the United States can do to reward Egypt for all it does strategically and politically for the United States in the region. There has always been resentment by the Egyptians that they play second fiddle to the Israelis. When Egypt was receiving $2.1 billion in aid from the United States, Israel was receiving $3 billion, and aid to Israel always had less strings attached than aid to Egypt. Moreover, freezing the military aid at $1.3 billion a year meant that in real terms (when adjusted for inflation), actual U.S. military assistance has been on a steady decline.[8]

Nonetheless, the bilateral military relationship has resulted in a couple of generations of Egyptian military officers receiving U.S. military education (at various professional military education (PME) institutions in the United States),[9] familiarization with U.S. military doctrine, and a generally favorable disposition toward the United States. Egypt's purchase of U.S. military hardware (which most of the military aid is used for) has resulted in better interoperability of forces between the two countries. Until recently, the United States and Egypt staged biennial military exercises called Bright Star on Egyptian soil,[10] and such exercises have assisted the United States in times of crisis, like the first Gulf war of 1990-91, when U.S. and Egyptian forces worked together in the effort to defend Saudi Arabia and roll back the Iraqi invasion of Kuwait.

Although the Cold War is over and Egypt may not be the cornerstone country it once was for U.S. strategic planners, the idea of "losing" Egypt as a strategic ally is not an attractive option for U.S. officials. At the very least, it would put the Arab-Israeli situation in jeopardy, contributing to instability in the region, and make it more difficult for the United States to confront security threats in the Horn of Africa and the Persian Gulf region.

THE CHALLENGE OF DEALING WITH DIFFERENT CENTERS OF POWER

Under Sadat, and later Mubarak, the United States had one address to which it went to get cooperation on various issues related to Middle Eastern affairs and security—that was, in essence, the presidential office. Sadat and Mubarak were the decisionmakers, parliament was largely a rubber stamp institution, the press and opposition figures were either co-opted or were on a short leash, and the military were subordinate to the president. Egyptian President Mubarak, for example, often took unpopular positions at home if he believed such positions would be beneficial for U.S.-Egyptian strategic ties and Egypt's position in the region, such as being the go-between for Israeli-Palestinian negotiations.

During the revolution of January-February 2011, the U.S. administration, after some initial hesitation, came to the conclusion that Mubarak had become a liability—the aged leader was unwilling to make significant changes to mollify his people—and the United States was willing to encourage the Egyptian military to convince Mubarak that it was time to step down.[11] The belief at the time was that the Egyptian military would shepherd the democratic transition, and this institution, being so powerful in its own right, would help to preserve the U.S.-Egyptian strategic relationship. Moreover, most of the young people who came to demonstrate in Tahrir Square did not espouse an anti-U.S. agenda but instead were calling for democratic government, which conformed to U.S. ideals. After Mubarak was toppled, the once-banned Muslim Brotherhood, because of its organizational strength and its history of opposition to the Mubarak regime, soon emerged as the most important political organization in Egypt, compelling U.S. policymakers to take notice and begin to cultivate ties to its leadership. Hence, when high-ranking U.S. officials came to Cairo in 2011, they made a point of visiting officials in the Brotherhood as well as the SCAF.[12] After the parliamentary elections of late 2011 and early 2012, the Brotherhood, winning about 47 percent of the seats, became the dominant party in that body and controlled not only the position of speaker but most of the parliamentary committees.

This "two-stop shopping" by U.S, officials — reaching out mainly to the military and the Brotherhood — had its limitations, however. It has had the unintended effect of convincing many Egyptian liberals — in many respects the natural allies of the United States — that the United States was very willing to deal with what they saw was Egypt's illiberal forces — the military and the Brotherhood — at the expense of the truly democratic forces.[13] This is a sentiment that was also shared by the young revolutionaries who mobilized their supporters in Tahrir Square in 2011 as well as political parties espousing liberal philosophies. When the Brotherhood appeared to overplay its hand in parliament in early 2012, tried to monopolize the constitution writing process, and appeared to do very little to improve the Egyptian economy, the Brotherhood's image among the general public fell. The liberals found an ally in the courts, which disbanded the assembly, picked largely by the Brotherhood to write the constitution, and later dissolved the lower house of parliament itself on technical grounds (arguing that the present configuration had violated the rule that one-third of the seats would be reserved for independent candidates).[14]

Be that as it may, U.S. policymakers continued to court the Egyptian military and the Brotherhood, even when bilateral relations went through a very difficult period, namely the late December 2011 crackdown on American and other foreign nongovernmental organizations (NGOs) that were involved in democracy promotion work. Although the instigator of this crackdown was probably a holdover from the Mubarak regime, Minister of International Cooperation Fayza Abouel Naga, the Egyptian military went along with the crackdown and initially showed no interest in resolving it.[15] Only after several weeks of phone calls from President Barack Obama and visits by the Chairman of the Joint Chiefs of Staff and senior members of Congress, along with threats to cut off U.S. military aid, did the SCAF relent and allow the American and other foreign NGO workers to leave Egypt, but it did not resolve the issue of the democracy promotion NGOs in Egypt themselves, which the Egyptian government saw as interference in their domestic affairs.[16]

The Egyptian military's initial reluctance to release the American NGO workers, including the son of the U.S. Secretary of Transportation who was working for the International Republican Institute and had taken refuge in the U.S. Embassy in Cairo, was probably because it was piqued that the U.S. administration had criticized it in the last months of 2011 because of the violence perpetrated against demonstrators in November and December. The U.S. Congress added language in the Fiscal Year (FY) 12 omnibus spending bill that was passed in late 2011 to the effect that the United States should withhold aid to Egypt unless the administration could certify that Egypt was meeting certain democratic benchmarks. After the United States paid roughly $5 million to Egypt for the release of its nationals in the NGO controversy, a Senate committee deducted $5 million from Egypt's economic support funds for FY 13 as a way of getting "some of our money back."[17] Meanwhile, when the Secretary of State exercised the national security waiver in the FY12 legislation to give Egypt the $1.3 billion in military aid (despite the fact that Egypt did not meet the democratic benchmarks in the legislation), some influential members of Congress, like Democratic Senator Patrick Leahy, chairman of the Senate Foreign Operations Subcommittee, sharply criticized the Obama administration for exercising this waiver.[18] Clearly, the U.S. administration believed that holding up military assistance to Egypt would damage its ties to the Egyptian military and was willing to buck congressional pressure to maintain these links.[19]

That said, the Obama administration was critical of what it believed was the Egyptian military's reluctance to give up power—especially following the presidential election in June 2012, which the SCAF had pledged earlier would be the time when the military would go back to the barracks. With the election results indicating that Muslim Brotherhood candidate Mohammed Morsi had won the presidential contest over a former military man, Ahmed Shafiq, the SCAF, on June 17, 2012, issued a constitutional declaration giving it vast powers (including legislative powers in the absence of a parliament) and severely limiting the powers of the new president. The new president would have no control over the military (and the military budget) and would not be authorized to declare war without the consent of the military.[20] This was widely seen in Egypt and in Washington not only as the military's attempt to keep power for itself but to keep the Brotherhood in check. During Secretary of State Hilary Clinton's visit to Egypt in mid-July, after Morsi was sworn in as president under these new edicts, Defense Minister Tantawi tried to justify the SCAF's moves by saying that "Egypt will never fall . . . to a certain group—the armed forces will not allow it."[21] However, Secretary Clinton stated publicly shortly before meeting with Tantawi and shortly after meeting with Morsi that the United States supports Egypt's "full transition to civilian rule," and the return of its military to a "purely national security role."[22] This was a U.S. signal that Washington was unhappy with the Egyptian military's apparent power grab, probably believing that prolonged military rule would lead to instability and strife. Even though Washington was probably not pleased that Egypt's new president came from the Muslim Brotherhood—with which it has had many differences over foreign policy issues—U.S. policymakers believed the outcome of the presidential election should be respected, and that the United States could have a good working relationship with Morsi. Later in the month, Defense Secretary Panetta visited Cairo and also had meetings with Morsi and Tantawi. Panetta mentioned publicly that Morsi "is his own man,"[23] suggesting that he was taking him at his word that he had resigned from the Brotherhood and was acting independently of any political faction. Panetta also said that Morsi and Tantawi appeared to have a good working relationship—which we now know in hindsight was not the case—given that Morsi forced Tantawi to retire only a couple of weeks later.

These episodes showed that the United States, despite its criticism of the Egyptian military, still pursued the policy of "two-stop shopping" it had begun months earlier. This may have been logical given the fact that the military was a known institution to the United States and the Brotherhood had emerged as the preeminent political organization in the country. However, as the first round of the Egyptian presidential elections showed, the Egyptian people's political preferences were varied.[24] In a divided field, several candidates of different political persuasions got almost the same number of votes. The two top vote-getters wound up being Mohammed Morsi, the Brotherhood candidate, and Ahmed Shafiq, the former air force commander, former minister of civil aviation and Mubarak's last prime minister. But both of these received only about 25 percent of the vote, hardly a ringing endorsement of their philosophies. The electorate was thus left with a choice of the Brotherhood or a former Mubarak regime official in the second round of voting, an unappealing prospect to many Egyptians.[25]

Moreover, the fact that Morsi edged out Shafiq in the second round of the presidential election did not mean that a majority of Egyptians had swung around and become Brotherhood supporters. Many Egyptians of liberal persuasion simply stayed home while Brotherhood supporters came out in strong numbers, and many of the young revolutionaries threw their support behind Morsi because they feared a return of the old regime if Shafiq won.[26] Hence, the second round of the presidential election was not a true indicator of the Egyptian people's political preferences.

Morsi, considered a rather lackluster candidate, nonetheless grew comfortable in his new job after he was sworn in as president on June 30, and when an opportunity arose to change the power configuration in the country, he quickly seized it. That opportunity was the killing of 16 Egyptian soldiers in the Sinai along the Egyptian-Israeli border on August 5, 2012. A group of Islamist extremists fired on the soldiers, stole their armored vehicles, and attempted to smash into the Israeli side of the border before being stopped by Israeli forces. In the aftermath of this incident, Morsi fired Egypt's intelligence chief and later proceeded to shake up the Egyptian military establishment. He issued orders to retire Tantawi, army chief of staff Anan, as well as the chiefs of the navy, air force, and air defense commands, and he replaced them with younger officers. Surprisingly to many in Egypt, the senior members of the military went along with these changes, and Morsi won an important political victory.[27] Although the complete story of this episode is not yet known, it appears that Morsi may have reached out to some younger members of the SCAF ahead of time to signal his intent, and so his moves were not a complete surprise.[28] He chose as his new defense minister a current member of the SCAF and the former military intelligence chief, General Abdel Fatah al-Sissi. Although Morsi's moves appeared radical, he did not choose a civilian to head up the defense ministry but someone from the defense establishment itself. Nor did he make any moves to rein in the military's autonomy or business interests. He probably figured that to move on these fronts at this stage would be a bridge too far. Instead, he settled on a shakeup of the military hierarchy. The fact that Tantawi and Anan were associated with many of the repressive policies of the SCAF's rule in 2011 and 2012 also allowed Morsi to score some points with the public, or at least with the activist youth groups who took part in the revolution.

More controversial during this time was Morsi's decision to assume both presidential and legislative powers that the military, under Tantawi, had claimed for itself just 2 months earlier. Morsi also moved against several media personalities who have been critical of him and the Brotherhood. The Shura Council, the upper body of parliament that was not disbanded by the courts and which has been dominated by the Brotherhood since the elections in the early spring of 2012, appointed pro-Brotherhood editors to head the government-owned newspaper. Many observers in Egypt believe that Morsi was personally involved in the decision to appoint these editors.[29]

For liberal-oriented Egyptians, Morsi won plaudits for his moves against an illiberal military hierarchy that had thrown thousands of Egyptians into prison since February 2011 and for his exertion of presidential control over the military.[30] However, these positive moves, in their view, were counterbalanced by his apparent power grab. The latter fed their worst fears about the Brotherhood. Morsi, in their view, was now acting in an authoritarian manner and might even try to influence the constitutional writing process through his proxies (like the military before him, he reserved the right to draft the new constitution if the body set to write it failed to do its job) as well as new parliamentary elections. Egyptian liberals keenly want the new constitution to reflect the ideals of a civic state in which all Egyptians are equal before the law and in which religion is not a deciding factor.[31] They also want to compete on a level playing field in the parliamentary elections. Although Morsi has officially re-signed from the Brotherhood, they fear he still wants to impose a narrow Islamist agenda on the country.

Hence, as of late August 2012, Egypt's political map encompasses Morsi as president, the military as a powerful institution behind the scenes, and many un-knowns—such as the political parties and factions that will control parliament in the near future. (Morsi has chosen a cabinet but his cabinet ministers are mostly made up of nonpowerful technocrats).[32] Although the Brotherhood and the more fundamentalist Salafi par-ties held a majority in parliament in early 2012 before that body was dissolved by the courts, it is not as-sured that they will get the same percentage of seats when the new parliament is elected. In late 2011 and early 2012, much of the Brotherhood's vote came from non-Brotherhood members willing to give this long-standing opposition party a try, and they did not like what they saw. For non-Brotherhood members, the Brotherhood was seen as trying to impose its will on the rest of parliament and monopolize not only parlia-ment's agenda but the constitutional writing process as well.[33] Hence, if the new parliamentary elections are free and fair, we can probably expect a drop in the Brotherhood's support from the 47 percent of the seats it won last time. Moreover, it is very possible that many Egyptians will vote strategically this time around. Facing a president originally from the Broth-erhood, many Egyptians will now want parliament not to be dominated by this same organization; hence, they may vote in a way to make parliament serve as a check on the president. They would want parliament to exercise significant power for this same reason. Finally, the judiciary is also an institution that bears watching. Morsi has appointed two brothers from the

Mekki family to his administration (they were outspoken judges against the Mubarak regime during the late Mubarak era). One, Mahmoud Mekki, has been appointed vice president, the other, Ahmed Mekki, has been appointed minister of justice. Although neither of them are members of the Muslim Brotherhood, they are believed to be sympathetic toward it.[34] Some Egyptians believe that Morsi made these selections to reform the judiciary, which still has many judges who were put in place during the Mubarak regime. However, the judiciary in Egypt is a respected institution and if Morsi is seen as trying to appoint like-minded judges (such as those sympathetic to the Muslim Brotherhood) to the higher courts, he runs the risk of a popular backlash. It remains to be seen what he and his new minister of justice will do.

THE NEW REGIME'S FOREIGN AND SECURITY POLICIES

Although Egypt's political picture is still a work in progress, there are already some trends underway that are affecting its foreign policy and security positions. The most immediate security concern facing Egypt (expressed by Morsi and the military) is the lawlessness of the Sinai and the extremist operations therein. The Egyptian military is taking the lead in bringing more military assets to the area to clamp down on the extremist groups, and there have already been clashes between the military and some of these extremists. On August 20, 2012, new Defense Minister General Abdel Fattah al-Sissi traveled to the northern Sinai to meet with disaffected Bedouin leaders to hear their complaints and to enlist their support against the extremists. Reportedly, al-Sissi offered rewards to the

Bedouin to collect weapons in the area. He also promised them that $165 million in development assistance would be given to the area.[35] The Egyptian government's strategy seems to be to peel off Bedouin support for the extremists and enlist them in the struggle to isolate and confront the extremists. Long neglected by Cairo, the Bedouin will probably take a wait-and-see approach until they observe actual assistance arriving from the central government. Most of the Bedouin in the Sinai are not religious fanatics, and some observers believe that those Bedouin youth who have joined the extremists have done so either for monetary reasons or because they had become susceptible to the extremists' message because of their own poor station in life. Hence, it makes sense for the Egyptian government and military to pursue this strategy, but only time will tell if it will actually work.

Press reports indicate that the U.S. military is also very interested in helping the Egyptians deal with the security situation in the Sinai. On August 14, 2012, the *Washington Post* reported that the U.S. administration is eager to enter discussions with the new Egyptian military leadership to chart a "collaborative plan to restore order in the restless Sinai." More broadly, a senior unnamed U.S. defense official was quoted in the same report as stating that U.S. military officials will also want to discuss with their Egyptian counterparts ways to make the Egyptian military into a more nimble force as opposed to reliance on heavy armor and war plans. To underscore Washington's interest in helping the Egyptian military, discussions have already started "to increase information sharing on a variety of issues and ways of cooperating even more."[36] On August 20, 2012, the Cable News Network (CNN) reported that the Pentagon is offering to supply Egypt's military in the Sinai with truck-mounted sensors that provide an electronic signal identifying which nation is operating the vehicle. These sensors can be used to identify vehicles at great distance. The same CNN report stated that the U.S. administration is also offering Egypt more intelligence sharing, including satellite imagery, drone flights and intercepts of cell phone and other communications among militants suspected of planning attacks in the Sinai. This offer is designed to help the Egyptian government improve security in the Sinai and to reassure the Israelis.[37]

Most likely, President Morsi and the Egyptian military will want to receive such assistance because they have come to believe the government must regain control over the Sinai, especially after its own soldiers were killed there in the extremist attack. However, making the Egyptian military into a nimble force is likely to be more problematic. As the U.S. experience with Pakistan has shown, perceptions of threats can be very different, even among friends. From Pakistan's perspective, India remains its major threat despite the terrorism and clashes it has encountered from the Taliban and like-minded groups. According to various press reports, the United States has for many years tried to get the Pakistani military to focus primarily on its northwest and western regions where extremists are active, rather than on its eastern frontier with India, but with little success.[38] Similarly, the Egyptian military still sees Israel as its major threat despite the fact that the two countries have been at peace for more than 30 years. Hence, while U.S. military officials are likely to find a receptive audience among the Egyptian military officers in finding ways to better detect and thwart extremist operations in the Sinai, they are likely to encounter resistance from the Egyptians on how they should view their long-term threats. Moreover, any U.S. suggestions to downsize their large standing army are also likely to encounter resistance. In the Egyptian view, downsizing spells weakness, especially when confronted by a more technologically advanced Israeli force. Additionally, a large force also contributes to their clout domestically in Egypt.

As for relations with Iran, Morsi is attempting to flex his muscles somewhat. For most of the Mubarak era, relations with Iran were either poor or nonexistent, not so much because Mubarak wanted to follow the U.S. lead but rather because he saw Iran and the Iranian revolution as antithetical to Egypt's national security interests. Morsi has already welcomed the Iranian vice president to Cairo, and he traveled to Tehran in late August 2012 to attend a meeting of the Non-Aligned Movement over U.S. objections.[39] Iran has signaled it has no opposition to a restoration of relations with Egypt, but it expects Cairo to take the initiative on this issue. Under a Morsi presidency, it is possible to expect somewhat of a warming of Egyptian-Iranian relations, but close ties are probably not in the offing. Indicative of this ambiguity, although Morsi was warmly received by the Iranian leadership when he arrived in Tehran, he gave a hard-hitting speech at the meeting against the Syrian regime—Iran's ally in the Arab world—much to the consternation of this same Iranian leadership.[40] Egypt also has other interests it needs to maintain, such as those with Saudi Arabia and the United States, which want to keep Iran boxed in and keep it from developing nuclear weapons. Too close a relationship with Iran might very well work to hinder U.S. and Saudi financial assistance to Egypt. Moreover, as a preeminent Sunni Muslim country, Egypt is never going to see eye-to-eye with Iran on many issues as long as a Shiite clerical regime rules from Tehran. Nonetheless, Egypt is likely to outwardly flirt with Iran to show, both for domestic and regional reasons, that it is pursuing an independent foreign policy. It should be remembered that this reaching out to Iran even occurred in the late Mubarak era—Egypt, during this period, received some Iranian diplomats as a way of showing independence from the United States when it was annoyed with U.S. policies on other issues.

On Israel, Egypt has no choice but to cooperate with Israel on security issues related to their common border, but on larger Israeli-Palestinian issues, Egypt will probably not play the helping hand that it did under the Mubarak regime. While Egypt remains committed to helping to secure a Palestinian modus vivendi between Hamas and Fatah,[41] and it tried to calm tensions between Israel and Hamas in June 2012,[42] it is not likely to play the middleman role it once did if that calls for real pressure on the Palestinians. One reason is that Egyptian diplomacy is likely to be more influenced by domestic public opinion than ever before, and the Egyptian public, whether Islamist or secularist, remains highly critical of Israel. Symptomatic of this sentiment, when Morsi received a congratulatory letter from Israeli President Shimon Peres on the occasion of the Muslim holy month of Ramadan and acknowledged it, news of the exchange became so controversial in Egypt that Morsi quickly denied that he had ever responded to the Peres letter.[43]

Egypt's relations with Israel during the Mubarak era were often characterized as a "Cold Peace." Nonetheless, Mubarak received many Israeli visitors and proved to be, more often than not, a helpful player in the peace process. It is hard to imagine at this stage that Morsi would receive Israeli official visitors. Although Morsi has pledged that he would respect all of Egypt's international treaties—implying the peace treaty with Israel—the Brotherhood has historically never supported the peace treaty, nor recognized the State of Israel. After the toppling of Mubarak, the Brotherhood, like several other political factions and political figures in Egypt, called for a revision of some of the treaty's terms, like the restrictions on Egyptian military deployments in the Sinai.[44] Ironically, as mentioned earlier, given the instability in the Sinai, even Israel has signaled that it would not be averse to some temporary, enhanced Egyptian security on its border as a way of dealing with the extremist menace, though this sentiment has its limits.[45] On August 21, 2012, Israeli officials charged that Egypt was violating the peace treaty by deploying tanks along the Israeli border. The press reported that, in the wake of the terrorist attack on Egyptian soldiers on August 5, Egypt deployed armored personnel carriers and attack helicopters to the area in coordination with the Israelis. But the subsequent Egyptian military deployments were apparently not coordinated with Israel, prompting Israeli concern. Press reports have indicated that the Israeli military sent several messages to the Egyptians about the latter deployments but received no response. One Israeli defense official was quoted as saying, "We must be very severe with abiding by the spirit and the letter of the peace treaty—otherwise we will be on a slippery slope, and no one knows where this might lead."[46] It seems that the Israelis objected on August 21 not because of Egypt's deployment of the tanks to the border area, but rather because they were not consulted about this move ahead of time.

With the Israeli-Palestinian peace process track essentially in abeyance and with relative calm between the Israelis and the Palestinians, Morsi does not have to make any difficult decisions on Egyptian policy toward the Israeli-Palestinian situation at this juncture. However, this situation could change overnight if a new flare-up occurs in Gaza between Hamas and Israeli forces. There are long, historical ties between Egypt's Muslim Brotherhood and Hamas; indeed, Hamas grew out of the Palestinian Muslim Brotherhood. If violence recurs between Israel and Gaza, it is possible that a Morsi presidency might allow for some military aid to be given to Hamas, which controls Gaza. The Egyptian military might initially resist such assistance, particularly because it might jeopardize the peace treaty between the two countries and lead to retaliatory Israeli strikes on Egypt that the Egyptian military would not be in a position to respond to and win. On the other hand, Egyptian popular pressure to assist the Palestinians might become so strong that the Egyptian military might feel that it has no choice but to assist the Palestinians. It should be remembered that during the last violent flare-up in early 2009, the Mubarak regime's decision to keep the Egyptian-Gaza border closed led to Egyptian public demonstrations and anger against the regime.[47] (It is important to note that after the completion of this monograph in August 2012, President Morsi did provide political, but not military, support to Hamas when violence recurred in the Fall of 2012.)

How does the United States maintain its influence in this changing environment? Given that Morsi and the military are still in an uneasy dance, the United States should still deal with both. Morsi is the democratically elected president of the country, and he should continue to be courted by U.S. officials. But it should be remembered that even though a strong presidency is part of Egyptian political culture, parliament is likely to have more powers than it had under the Mubarak regime. Although much depends on how the new constitution will be written and the delineation of powers that will be in that document, it is probably safe to assume that parliament will not be the rubber stamp institution that it was in the past under Mubarak. This means it will likely weigh in strongly on domestic and foreign policy issues. As such, U.S. policymakers should meet with the majority party or factions within parliament as well as with the opposition. This would not only signal U.S. support for democracy and Egypt's legislative body, but will help to develop relations with parties and political figures who might come to power in the future. Indeed, if Egypt develops into a democracy or even a quasi-democracy where presidents and parliaments are subject to free and fair elections (implying a turnover of power), relying on merely the president and the military would be shortsighted.

Finally, Egypt has long wanted to reclaim its leadership role in the Arab world, and Egyptians of all political persuasions believe this is a natural role for the country to play.[48] Given Egypt's current economic problems (zero growth, depletion of foreign exchange reserves, and high unemployment) as well as its unsettled political situation, it is not in a position to do so now, but for many Egyptians this is just a temporary condition. Once Egypt puts its economic and political house in order, the thinking goes, it will be ready to lead the Arab world again. This type of thinking may seem more of a pipe dream at this point, but it may come to pass down the road. This positioning may put

Egypt at odds with Saudi Arabia which, with the support of the much smaller state of Qatar, tried to act as a leader of the Arab world in the past decade. This is most evident in relation to the ongoing Syrian crisis. Although Egypt and Saudi Arabia often see eye-to-eye on many regional issues, there is also tension and rivalry beneath the surface.[49] This will be a challenge for U.S. policymakers as they try to navigate between these two competitors for Arab leadership in the years ahead.

EGYPTIAN POLITICAL SCENARIOS AND U.S. STRATEGIC INTERESTS

Although the discussion above has outlined likely Egyptian foreign and security policies in the months and years ahead, much also depends on how Egyptian politics are settled, the powers of various institutions in the country, the relationship between the president and the military and parliament, and the outcome of the parliamentary elections. The following section discusses various scenarios and explores how each of them will affect U.S. strategic interests.

Scenario I.

President Morsi acts as a democratic leader for all Egyptians and does not interfere with the constitutional drafting process and parliamentary elections, allowing secular-liberal and leftist groups to win seats and share power with Islamists in that body. Morsi also allows the Egyptian military to retain its autonomy.

This scenario is probably the best outcome for Egypt's democratic advancement. Morsi does not pursue a narrow Islamist agenda despite his Muslim Brotherhood background but instead tries to act above party politics. His main concerns are to see that the constitution drafting process is fair (allowing Egypt's diverse political factions to feel that they are part of the process and not excluded), that parliamentary elections take place without presidential bias toward Muslim Brotherhood candidates, and that parliament becomes an equal branch of government. Concerning the military, Morsi will try to influence matters through his handpicked Defense Minister but will not interfere in the military's policies except to free Egyptians who were imprisoned during SCAF's reign (something he is already doing). He will likely preside over weekly meetings of the national defense council to show that he is in charge, but he will not interfere in the military's expenditures and priorities. The military will take the lead in pacifying the Sinai and in cooperating with the Israelis on border issues but will keep Morsi informed about these developments. Given Egypt's severe economic problems, Morsi will have his hands full trying to revitalize the Egyptian economy while adhering to International Monetary Fund (IMF) conditions that will accompany the expected IMF loan and will not pursue an adventurous foreign policy. He will not extend a helping hand to the Israelis in the peace process but neither will he pursue an antagonistic policy toward Israel.

Under this scenario, U.S. strategic relations with Egypt are largely maintained. Morsi would not act in a way that would jeopardize the annual $1.3 billion in U.S. military assistance approved by Congress. Egypt would continue to grant access to U.S. military aircraft and naval ships moving through its air and sea lanes, and Egyptian officers would continue to come to the

United States for training. Any cooperation with the United States and Israel on Sinai security issues will probably be discussed under the radar screen to avoid any public backlash. Although the Egyptian military would still be an institution operating "off the books" in terms of budget issues, Morsi would countenance that as long as the military does not interfere in domestic politics. Parliament would represent the Egyptian public's diverse political sentiments and would not pursue a strict Islamist agenda that many in Washington would see as hurting minority and women's rights. Egypt would be seen as a success in terms of democratic transition and may be rewarded by the U.S. Congress with additional economic assistance. Although relations with Israel would be maintained, Egypt would not likely be an intermediary between the Palestinians and the Israelis. But as long as no outbreak of violence occurs, continued maintenance of a cold peace would be as much as could be expected under a Muslim Brotherhood presidency.

Scenario II.

Morsi becomes an authoritarian leader, clamps down on dissent, purges the judiciary and the press of critics of the Brotherhood, and influences the drafting of the constitution and the parliamentary elections to favor the Brotherhood's Islamist agenda and its ideology. He allows the military, however, to retain its autonomy and does not interfere with their operations or their interests.

Under this scenario, U.S. security interests would also be preserved, at least initially, but at a price. Morsi would concentrate on domestic matters to pursue a narrow Islamist agenda and would generally leave the military alone. Democracy would be compromised, as he would concentrate power in the hands of the presidency and try to bring parliament, which would be dominated by the Brotherhood, under his control. Although lip service would be given to the separation of powers, in essence the Brotherhood, through Morsi as president, would have a near monopoly of political life in the country. Minority rights and women's rights would be curtailed, social restrictions would be imposed on Egyptian citizens, and his critics would be thrown in jail under the presidency's control of the Ministry of Interior's police forces. Morsi would leave the defense and security realm to the military, and because he would not interfere with military matters, he would in essence be striking a deal with that institution. The military would want to maintain their links with the United States and to keep peace with the Israelis (especially in terms of securing the Sinai), and it would bank on the fact that the United States, wishing to preserve these security links, would overlook the authoritarian nature of the government. It would not be a stretch for the Egyptian military to think this way because for decades under Sadat and Mubarak, the United States did its best to downplay the authoritarian nature of these governments for geo-strategic interests. However, it is highly likely that the U.S. Congress would not countenance a close relationship with Egypt under these circumstances. If Morsi does become an authoritarian leader and works to make Egypt an Islamist state that curtails minority and women's rights, it is conceivable that Congress would reduce or cut off aid to Egypt; even the military aid that has been the backbone of the relationship. Although there would be countervailing pressures from elements in the U.S. administration arguing such draconian measures would cut the links with the one pro-U.S. institution remaining in the country and be counterproductive, Congress would likely prevail in this struggle as influential members argue that the United States should not reward authoritarianism that in some respects would be worse than the Mubarak regime. With U.S. withdrawal of support to the Egyptian military, U.S. security links to the Egyptian military—along with overflight and refueling stops for U.S. military aircraft—would be adversely affected.

Scenario III.

Morsi becomes an authoritarian leader and pursues a narrow Islamist agenda that gives the Brotherhood a monopoly of power over all major institutions in the country. He also takes firmer control over the military, clamps down on the military's autonomy, and purges the officer corps of those not sympathetic to the Brotherhood's agenda. He pursues an aggressive foreign policy that openly sides with Hamas and other Islamist groups in the region. While not embarking on war with Israel, he declares that the Israeli-Egyptian peace treaty is no longer valid and openly funnels arms to Hamas in the Gaza Strip. He also openly disagrees with Saudi Arabia about regional security threats.

This would be a worst-case scenario for U.S. security interests. Not only would Morsi scuttle the hopes for a democratic transition in Egypt—jeopardizing continued U.S. assistance—but he would embark on a policy that would change the nature and ideology of the Egyptian military to the point where it would not be inclined to maintain links to the U.S. military. Although a major purge of the officer corps would take time and there would be vestiges of pro-U.S. sentiment within the military for some time, a comprehensive and transformative shake up of the military would likely end the close collaboration between U.S. and Egyptian military services that has been in existence for the past 30 years. The United States would lose access and overflight rights, and could not count on Egypt for assistance in case of major security challenges in the Persian Gulf. On the Palestinian-Israeli front, although Morsi, under this scenario, would not want to start a war with Israel given the likelihood that Egypt would lose the Sinai again, if he does take an active role to aid Hamas militarily, the Israelis might conclude that it would be in their interests to strike Egypt first, as it did in 1967. Even a mini-war between Israel and Egypt would have untold regional consequences, perhaps drawing other countries and parties into the conflict. Because it would lack leverage with the Egyptians, the United States would be powerless to stop such a war from happening. Although conventional thinking is that the United States would have enough clout to stop an Israeli attack on Egypt, if Israel believes that its security is threatened by a revanchist Egypt, no amount of U.S. pressure would deter the Israelis if they felt their security would be on the line.

How Does the United States Optimize Its Leverage to See that Scenario I Comes to Pass Instead of Scenarios II or III?

It is in the U.S. national security interest to have Egypt become a democratic state where basic freedoms are respected, checks and balances between government institutions are developed, and the

United States maintains close links to the Egyptian military. Although democracy will mean that public opinion will be much more of a factor in the formation of Egyptian foreign and security policies in ways it has not been before—making relations with the United States and Israel even more controversial than they were in the past—the alternative to democracy is more problematic. A return to authoritarian government, especially one with a narrow Islamist agenda that would impose prohibitions against alcohol and western-style dress for women and limit opportunities for its Coptic Christian minority would hurt the return of tourism and foreign investment to the country, lead to increased sectarian strife in Egypt, and dash the hopes of Egypt's younger generation, many of whom put their lives on the line in 2011 to bring down the Mubarak authoritarian regime in favor of democratic government. For this reason, on the political level, the U.S. policymakers should continue to emphasize that the new rulers of Egypt should respect the universal norms of freedom of assembly, press, and religion, and that minority and women's rights should also be respected in whatever new constitution Egypt adopts. At the same time, the United States should stay away from the very sensitive issue of the role of religion and sharia (Islamic law) in the new constitution because that is for the Egyptians themselves to decide, and whatever comments the United States makes on those issues would likely backfire in any case.

Ideally, with a former Muslim Brotherhood official now in control of the presidency, it would be in the interest of Egypt (and the U.S.) for the yet-to-be elected parliament not to be under the Brotherhood's sway. Having control over both the presidency and parliament might tempt more hard-line elements in the Brotherhood to seize the opportunity and push through legislation that would change the nature of Egypt and its liberal traditions. Although a significant minority of Egyptians would be happy living under a strict Islamist state, a majority of Egyptians—who tend to see religion as a personal matter and not something that should be imposed by the state—would not. It should be remembered that in a divided presidential field, as was the case of the first round of the presidential elections in May 2012, Morsi only received about 25 percent of the vote. Presumably, the other 75 percent of Egyptians do not want to be under a Muslim Brotherhood-dominated regime. In some respects, Morsi is smart enough to understand this, and for this reason he resigned from the Brotherhood and has since tried to reinvent himself as a democratic nationalist working for the interests of "all Egyptians."

However, it would be counterproductive for the United States to try to influence the outcome of the parliamentary elections by favoring one political faction over another. The favored faction would be labeled an American lackey and may lose public support because Egyptians are very sensitive to outside interference. What U.S. policymakers can do is to continue to call for such elections to be free and fair without one party having an unfair advantage over the field. This would be in line with universal democratic norms. When U.S. foreign policy and defense officials visit Egypt, they should be open to visit all political parties and factions, and not just spend their time courting the military and the Brotherhood (and the president). Such "two-stop shopping" gives the impression in Egypt that the United States has cut a deal with the Brotherhood and the military and does not care about the fate of the other groups. Secondly, some of these groups and political figures might emerge as leaders of the country one day, and it would be foolish not to treat them as equals, such as visiting them in their own party headquarters. After all, when U.S. officials visit European capitals, they often visit with opposition leaders in addition to host government officials. As a practical matter, if Morsi is not successful in turning the Egyptian economy around, he might be voted out of office in the next presidential election. The United States should not want to be in a position where it has no history of contacts with the next Egyptian president or for that winner to hold a grudge against the United States because it was ignored by U.S. officials in the preceding years.

Although conventional wisdom posits that divided government can lead to gridlock (and we know this from the U.S. experience), in Egypt's case it can lead to compromise and buy-in. If the parliamentary elections lead to no one faction dominating the parliamentary assembly, then Morsi and all of the factions within parliament would have to work together to fashion legislation that would be reflective of the Egyptian body politic. A strong and representative parliament could serve as a check on a president who may or may not have authoritarian tendencies.

As for the Egyptian military, it is entirely proper for U.S. policymakers to continue to say that this institution should return to its role of defending the nation. After all, this is what the Egyptian military has long said it wanted to do, and it is something that is taught in courses for foreign military officers (including Egyptian ones) in various professional military education (PME) institutions in the United States. The United States should deal with the Egyptian military in their traditional roles by participating in joint military exercises, holding discussions about regional security threats, and helping them deal with immediate security threats such as the extremist presence in the Sinai. Now that Morsi has taken away the military's political role and the military has acquiesced to this change, relations between the U.S. and Egyptian militaries can go back to their more natural condition, as they were before the revolution of early 2011.

Although language on U.S. aid to Egypt in the new Senate Foreign Operations Subcommittee bill states that Egypt must "provide civilian control over, and public disclosure of, the military and police budget," this will likely be a decision for Egypt's new president and its yet-to-be elected parliament to figure out. Down the road they will have to deal with such questions as: Will the military's budget continue to be secret or will it be subject to open debate? Will the military continue to be able to run their own businesses and farms? Will military officers continue to enjoy perquisites without civilian scrutiny? Although the military's wings have been clipped by Morsi who, in essence, has forced the military to return to the barracks, he and the new parliamentarians that are to be elected later in the year might believe they need to tread carefully on military budget and military transparency issues so as not to provoke a military backlash.

Although some Egypt analysts have called for a revamping of the U.S.-Egyptian relationship—making it less heavily dependent on the military (and U.S. military assistance),[50] other analysts have argued that cutting military aid would signal a lessening of U.S. support for Egypt and would wind up undermining U.S. influence in the country.[51]

With the political situation in Egypt still so unsettled, it is probably not wise to change the aid configuration—which is heavily tilted toward the military—at this time. A cut in military aid would likely be interpreted in Egypt as a signal that the United States was losing its interest in Egypt, which would have the potential to hinder or even to end U.S. access rights in Egypt, especially at a time when another crisis in the Persian Gulf may be brewing. Moreover, with Israel receiving about $3.1 billion annually in U.S. military aid, the perception in Egypt would be that the United States would now be even more biased toward Israel than in the current situation.

That said, it would also make sense for the United States to boost civilian aid to Egypt at this time, particularly when the Egyptian economy is in such dire straits. As of this writing, subcommittees in the U.S. House and Senate have approved $1.3 billion in military aid (foreign military financing), but only $250 million in economic support funds for FY 13, roughly the same amounts that Egypt has been receiving for the past few years. Both the Senate and House bills contain conditionality on this aid, and they will jointly have to arrive at common language before the spending bill is approved. The Senate bill contains conditionality on the military aid (though with a national security waiver), stating that the Secretary of State must certify that the government in Cairo is democratically elected and is implementing policies to: 1) provide civilian control over, and public disclosure of, the police and military budgets; 2) fully repeal the Emergency Law; and, 3) protect judicial independence, freedom of expression, association, assembly, and religion; the right of political opposition parties, civil society organizations, and journalists to operate without harassment or interference; and due process of law. The House bill says that both military aid and economic support funds are restricted until the Secretary of State certifies that Egypt is meeting its obligations under the Israeli-Egyptian peace treaty; has completed the transition to civilian government, including holding free and fair elections; and is implementing policies that protect freedom of expression, association, and religion, and due process of law.[52]

While such conditionality reflects the mood of the Congress to press Egypt to uphold democratic values and pursue policies that would be in line with these values, the United States would have a lot more influence with the Egyptian government if such conditionality were attached to substantially more civilian aid. There is a possibility that Egypt might receive additional aid from other U.S. foreign aid accounts. For example, the Senate bill approves $1 billion for a "Middle East and North Africa Incentive Fund," which could be used in part to fund education, investment, and small enterprises in Egypt as well as a reduction in Egypt's debt, but the House bill contains no such funding. Instead, the House bill approves $200 million for "Middle East Response," which includes $175 million for economic assistance and $25 million for military assistance, but there is no separate language on Egypt.[53] It is difficult to know how the two bills will be reconciled in conference and what additional money, if any, will go toward Egypt.

Although the United States faces budget constraints, and many members of Congress are not inclined to increase foreign assistance expenditures, a compelling case can be made to the Congress by administration officials on why such aid is needed for a country like Egypt. Administration officials should not argue against conditionality placed on the aid by Congress because it sends a signal to Egypt that the United States takes seriously the importance of respecting democratic norms. On the other hand, by

not helping Egypt in this difficult transition period —
politically and economically — with additional aid,
the United States might send the wrong signal about
the U.S. commitment to Egypt's future. As mentioned
earlier, events in Egypt are closely watched by other
peoples in the Arab world, and it was not a coinci-
dence that other movements in other countries expe-
riencing the Arab Spring tried to replicate the Tahrir
Square phenomenon in their own countries.[54] U.S.
military assistance to help Egyptian security forces
in the Sinai would certainly be appreciated by the
Egyptian military, but what would count more for
the Egyptian people is tangible U.S. assistance to
help the struggling Egyptian economy, particularly
in ways that try to tackle the very serious unemployment problem for Egypt's younger generation. Such
additional assistance would go a long way toward
generating goodwill.

At the same time, the United States should avoid
efforts to make the Egyptian military a "more nimble"
force. This is a losing proposition and will be interpreted as a way of weakening the Egyptian military,
feeding conspiracy theories about some nefarious U.S.
plot hatched in conjunction with Israel. Although it
may make sense to make the Egyptian military into a
leaner, more mobile force to respond to terrorist plots
and other contingencies, the political downsides of
such a proposition are so great as to make the effort
not worth pursuing.

Instead, U.S. policymakers should concentrate on
areas of cooperation (like Sinai security) and should
resume joint-training exercises that are valued by both
militaries.[55] These measures will underscore to Egypt
that the United States is respectful of and is eager to
help Egypt protect its national sovereignty, and they
will earn the United States the goodwill that is crucial

when a regional crisis necessitates Egypt's cooperation. During the first Gulf War of 1990-91, for example, Egypt not only played an important political role opposing Iraq's invasion of Kuwait, but its strategic decision to open its air corridors and bases for refueling stops for thousands of U.S. military aircraft played a crucial role in the war to reverse Iraq's aggression.[56] Although for political reasons, one can envision under a Morsi presidency that Egypt might not play such a politically supportive role if another crisis breaks out in the Gulf (such as one involving Iran), close military-to-military contacts and goodwill might enable strategic cooperation, especially if it is largely out of the public spotlight.

Nonetheless, there are likely to be challenges in the U.S.-Egyptian bilateral relationship in the years ahead now that Egypt is under new presidential leadership. The United States cannot count on Egypt to do any heavy lifting in the peace process unless the parties are very close to a deal that is satisfactory to the Palestinians. Morsi is not likely to push the Palestinians, for example, to accept an Israeli offer if Hamas comes out against it. He would lose credibility with his former colleagues in the Brotherhood and would also likely be criticized by secular-nationalists within Egypt. The most the United States can expect from Egypt within the next few years is to maintain the peace treaty with Israel and keep up efforts aimed at Palestinian reconciliation. Such efforts might serve to moderate Hamas's stance if Hamas moves closer to Fatah on peace process issues, but Egypt would not want to be seen pressuring Hamas in the process.

Concerning Iran, an Israeli or U.S. strike aimed at damaging its nuclear capabilities would also pose a challenge for the bilateral U.S.-Egyptian relationship.

Some members of the Egyptian officer corps might welcome such a strike, as they probably believe, like many Arab security officials in the Gulf countries, that Iran poses a security challenge to the region. However, public opinion in Egypt would likely view a strike in negative terms. Even though many Egyptians are opposed to Iran and its type of government,[57] they seem to admire its belligerent positions against Israel and its stance of defying the United States. This is probably one of the reasons Morsi decided to attend the Non-Aligned Movement summit in Tehran. In terms of Iran's nuclear question, although many Egyptians do not want a nuclear arms race in the region—which an Iranian nuclear weapons capability would likely trigger—they have long been upset about Israel's purported nuclear arsenal and see a double-standard in the response by the United States about this issue.[58] Hence, it is likely that a strike by either Israel or the United States on Iran would generate anti-Israeli and anti-U.S. demonstrations in Egypt. The Egyptian political leadership would likely side with the demonstrators even though such a stance would not be welcomed by either Washington or Riyadh, and such a strong public stand would make the Egyptian military skittish about cooperating with the United States, even in terms of access rights, fearing that such cooperation could become public. There is also the possibility that Morsi could use the strike to embarrass the Egyptian military if it does cooperate with U.S. defense officials in such an endeavor, though Morsi would have to be careful about how he would play this because, as president of the country, he is at least nominally in charge of the military.

Preserving the U.S.-Egyptian strategic partnership under Egypt's new regime is thus going to be a challenge for U.S. policymakers in the months and years ahead. Much depends on how Egypt's new president acts, how the U.S. Congress responds to his actions, and the powers and policies of Egypt's parliament once it is elected. Egypt's military will want to preserve the strategic relationship, but will have to be mindful of Morsi's policies as well as Egyptian public opinion. U.S. policymakers will also have to be mindful that the strategic partnership will be different than it was under Mubarak, and there will be times when either Egypt's new leaders or public opinion will pose limits on this partnership. However, there are enough common interests between the two countries to preserve this partnership if both sides handle relations with a good deal of patience, dexterity, and finesse.

RECOMMENDATIONS FOR THE U.S. ARMY

The following suggestions for the U.S. Army will preserve and enhance the bilateral security relationship during Egypt's current transition period:

1. Continue military-to-military contacts. The military relationship between the United States and Egypt has been a key component of the overall bilateral relationship since the late 1970s, and these ties have served as a steady keel in the relationship even when political problems arose between Cairo and Washington.

2. Continue to encourage Egyptian military officers to attend PME institutions in the United States. Such training gives Egyptian officers exposure to the United States (its people, culture, and politics) as well as U.S. military doctrine, and allows them the intellectual freedom to engage in discussions with their U.S. counterparts (and other foreign military officers attending the same institutions) on a variety of regional issues. Such educational opportunities also allow U.S. army officers to learn more about Egyptian culture

and military doctrine. In addition, the development of personal contacts between U.S. and Egyptian army officers, which such schooling provides, can enhance bilateral military cooperation, especially when regional crises arise.

3. Engage in high-level discussions with Egyptian military officials on regional threat perceptions. Although such discussions took place fairly regularly during the Mubarak era, they have been held only sporadically since then, as the Egyptian military hierarchy has concentrated on running the country and been annoyed at U.S. criticism of its domestic policies, according to various press reports. Now that Egyptian presidential elections have been held, a new military leadership is in place, and the military has essentially gone back to the barracks, it is time to restore such high-level discussions. These talks would help to reassure the Egyptian military that the United States shares many of its regional security concerns, and would work toward keeping the discussions on a professional military level as opposed to the more problematic political level when the SCAF ran the country.

4. Reactivate the Bright Star exercises. These biennial exercises were a mainstay of the relationship for more than 2 decades, as they allowed the Egyptian and U.S. militaries to engage in joint training exercises on Egyptian soil. They underscored the U.S. commitment to Egypt's defense and played an important role in the first Gulf war (1990-91) when the U.S. and Egyptian armies worked together to roll back the Iraqi invasion of Kuwait. Although given the new political dynamics in Egypt, approval of such exercises would have to go through President Morsi's office. However, he may not be averse to reactivating Bright Star, perhaps seeing it as a way of mollifying the Egyptian military and assuring the United States that there would be no

dramatic turn in Egypt's foreign affairs and security posture. Such a decision on Egypt's part to hold these exercises may not be made until after Egypt finishes its political transition, which includes new parliamentary elections in late 2012 or early 2013. In the meantime, the U.S. Army should continue to encourage the Egyptian military to participate in regional military exercises, as it did in Jordan earlier this year.[59]

5. Continue to offer to provide the Egyptian military with intelligence and sophisticated equipment to deal with the extremist threat in the Sinai. According to press reports, U.S. defense officials have offered the Egyptian military such tools to better monitor and detect terrorist threats in the troublesome Sinai.[60] In the aftermath of the August 2012 killing of 16 Egyptian soldiers along the Israeli-Egyptian border of the northern Sinai, the Egyptian political and military establishment has taken this threat much more seriously than in the past. The U.S. offer of help was probably well-received by the Egyptian army, but for domestic political reasons, it needs to show that it is acting alone to confront the extremist menace. The U.S. military can also play a behind-the-scenes role to deflate Egyptian-Israeli tensions over the Sinai by encouraging the Egyptian military to notify the Israelis in advance before they bring more military assets to the border region to confront the extremists.

At the same time, the U.S. Army should *avoid* engagement in the following areas, as they will likely hurt the bilateral relationship:

1. Discussions about Egyptian domestic politics and the Muslim Brotherhood. U.S. army officers should be made to understand that this is a very sensitive time in Egypt's history. Some Egyptian military officers are probably still upset over President Morsi's

"retirement" of the SCAF's old guard as well as the fact that Morsi, a former Muslim Brotherhood official, is now leader of the country. Other Egyptian military officers have probably come to grips with this new political reality and, as loyal officers of the state, believe they should cooperate with Morsi. Still others may have strong views about the new constitution, parliament, and the delineation of powers. In discussions with Egyptian military officers about regional security threats, U.S. Army officers should avoid any discussions about domestic politics and keep the talks in the realm of military and security spheres even if some of their Egyptian counterparts are inclined to venture into political topics. It is for the Egyptian public to decide who should be their political leaders, and any comments by U.S. military officers would not only be inappropriate but would likely backfire, as they would be used by one faction against another and ultimately harm U.S. interests. For example, if it appeared that a U.S. Army officer was agreeing with a disgruntled Egyptian military officer who espoused negative views about Morsi, word would probably get back to Morsi and his allies in the military and feed conspiracy theories about the United States trying to hatch a coup in Egypt. At the same time, if a pro-Brotherhood military officer started to denigrate Egyptian secular-liberal politicians and a U.S. army officer appeared to agree with that position, word of such an exchange might leak out and feed conspiracy theories already prevalent in Egypt about the United States cutting a deal with the Brotherhood.[61] Sticking to discussions about military matters is the only safe and appropriate path to follow for U.S. military officers.

2. Discussions about downsizing the Egyptian military and making it a seemingly more effective force. As mentioned earlier, press reports have suggested

that U.S. defense officials are interested in discussing with their Egyptian counterparts ways to make the Egyptian military a more nimble force. Although U.S. defense officials may sincerely believe such changes to the Egyptian military will be in Egypt's long-term national interests, the Egyptian officer corps will likely see such suggestions in a very negative light. A large standing army, albeit with lots of inefficiencies, nonetheless has advantages in the mindset of the Egyptian officer corps: it serves as a deterrent to its neighbors who may harbor ill-will against Egypt in the future; it serves to balance, to some degree, the Israeli military's technological advantage over Egypt; it serves to enhance the military's clout in Egyptian society; it makes the Egyptian military (with its businesses and farms) self-sufficient in many ways and not dependent on civilian politicians for budgetary support; and it helps take youth, who would otherwise be unemployed, off the streets for a couple of years and inculcates them with beliefs, such as respect for the military and establishment Islam (as opposed to an extremist version) that works in the interest of Egyptian stability. Given these strong beliefs held by the Egyptian officer corps, it would be counterproductive for U.S. Army officers to engage with their Egyptian counterparts in discussions, while well-intentioned, that even remotely suggests a downsizing of the Egyptian military.

ENDNOTES

1. The Supreme Council of the Armed Forces (SCAF), on its Facebook page, called the shake up a "natural change" and said the "responsibility has been moved to a new generation of Egypt's sons. . . ." See Ernesto Londono, "Egypt reacts with respect to president's new power," *Washington Post*, August 14, 2012.

2. Esam al-Amin, "Egyptian Military Checkmated," available from *www.counterpunch.org/2012/08/24/egyptian-military-checkmated/.*

3. *Ibid.* Estimates of the Egyptian military's role in the economy range from 5 to 40 percent. See also David D. Kirkpatrick, "Egyptians Say Military Discourages an Open Economy," *New York Times*, February 17, 2011.

4. Ernesto Landono and Joel Greenberg, "Sinai militants kill 15 Egyptian troops," *Washington Post*, August 6, 2012. See also Michael Herzog, "Sinai's Emergence as a Strategic Threat to Israel," available from *www.washingtoninstitute.org/policy-analysis/view/sinais-emergence-as-a-strategic-threat-to-Israel.*

5. GAO, Report to the Committee on International Relations, House of Representatives, "Security Assistance. State and DOD Need to Assess How the Foreign Military Financing Program for Egypt Achieves U.S. Foreign Policy and Security Goals," Washington, DC: U.S. Government Accountability Office, April 2006, p. 17.

6. Gregory L. Aftandilian, *Egypt's Bid for Arab Leadership: Implications for U.S. Policy*, New York: Council on Foreign Relations, 1993, pp. 21-28.

7. *Ibid.*, pp. 65-66.

8. See Steven Cook's interview on PBS on January 2, 2012. He stated: "If you do the math, it's [U.S. military aid to Egypt] worth 40 or 50 percent of what it once was." Available from *www.pbs.org/newshour/bb/world/jan-june12/egypt2_01-02.html.*

9. For example, both the new defense minister, General Abdel Fatah al-Sissi, and the new army chief of staff, General Sedky Sobhi, studied at the U.S. Army War College. See this reference in David Kirkpatrick, "In Paper, Chief of Egypt's Army Criticized U.S.," *New York Times*, August 16, 2012.

10. "Star Loses Magnitude," *Al-Ahram Weekly*, November 8-14, 2007.

11. Martin S. Indyk, Kenneth G. Lieberthal, Michael E. O'Hanlon, *Bending History: Barak Obama's Foreign Policy*, Washington, DC: Brookings Institution Press, 2012, p. 145.

12. "U.S. met with Egypt Islamists: U.S. diplomat," available from *www.reuters.com/article/2011/10/02/us-egypt-usa-brotherhood-idUSTRE7910J420111002*.

13. Comments from the Carnegie Endowment for International Peace seminar, "A Discussion with Amr Hamzawy," Washington, DC, May 4, 2012. Hamzawy is the president and founder of the Egyptian Freedom Party, one of Egypt's liberal parties.

14. Borzou Daraghi, "Egypt court orders parliament dismissed," *Financial Times*, June 15, 2012.

15. See Shadi Hamid, "Beyond Guns and Butter: A U.S.-Egyptian Relationship for a Democratic Era," Brookings Middle East Memo, April 2012, available from *www/brookings.edu/~/media/Files/rc/papers/2012/04_egypt_hamid/04_egypt_hamid.pdf*. See also, Denis Sullivan, "Will Egypt and the US Let the 'Filul' Win?" Atlantic Council, February 10, 2012, available from *www.acus.org/egyptsource/will-egypt-and-us-let-filul-win-o*

16. Ernesto Landono and William Wan, "Americans sheltered in U.S. Embassy," *Washington Post*, January 30, 2012.

17. Project on Middle East Democracy (POMED), "The Department of State, Foreign Operations, and Related Programs: Appropriations Bills, FY 13," p. 14.

18. Susan Cornwell and Arshad Mohammed, "Clinton to let military aid to Egypt go ahead, Leahy says," *Reuters*, March 22, 2012, available from *af.reuters.com/article/worldNews/idAFBRE82L12F20120322*.

19. Steven Lee Myers, "Once Imperiled, U.S. Aid to Egypt is Restored," *New York Times*, March 23, 2012.

20. Nathan Brown, "The Egyptian Political System in Disarray," *Commentary*, Washington, DC: Carnegie Endowment for International Peace, June 19, 2012, available from *www.carnegieendowment.org/2012/06/19/egyptian-political-system-in-disarray/c073*.

21. Hamza Hendawi, "Egypt's top general signals military won't give free rein to Brotherhood," *Washington Post*, July 16, 2012.

22. Stephanie McCrummon and Steve Hendrix, "In Cairo Clinton Says U.S. Backs Civilian Rule in Egypt," *Washington Post*, July 15, 2012.

23. Karen DeYoung, "From alarm to relief in Washington," *Washington Post*, August 14, 2012.

24. "Relive vote count in 1st round of Egypt presidential race: How Morsi and Shafiq moved on," *Ahram Online*, May 25, 2012, available from *english.ahram.org.eg/News/42755.aspx*.

25. Ian Black, "Egyptian election results present 'nightmare scenario,'" *The Guardian*, May 25, 2012.

26. Leila Fadel and Ernesto Landono, "Optimism waning, Egyptians making choice for president," *Washington Post*, June 17, 2012.

27. Ernesto Landono, "Egypt reacts with respect to president's new power," *Washington Post*, August 14, 2012.

28. Essam al-Amin, "Egypt's Military Checkmated."

29. "Journalists continue to protest against chief editors," *Egypt Independent*, August 15, 2012.

30. Mohammed El-Baradei, the former IAEA chief and Nobel prize winner who returned to Egypt as a liberal reformer, for example, praised the military shuffle, calling it a "step in the right direction." See Haroon Siddique and Louisa Loveluck, "Egypt reacts after Morsi moves against military chiefs," *The Guardian*, August 13, 2012.

31. See "Hamzawy reveals dispute in Constituent Assembly over identity of state," *ElYom7*, August 17, 2012. The article notes that Morsi's "consolidation of both legislative and executive powers is unacceptable and raises further concerns over the monopo-

45

lization of power by one faction." See also, "As Brotherhood consolidates power, Egypt loses 'guarantor of civil state,'" *Democracy Digest*, August 14, 2012.

32. Samer al-Atrush, "Egypt premier unveils new cabinet," AFP, August 1, 2012.

33. Mohamed Fade Fahmy, "Court disbands Egypt's constitutional group," CNN, April 11, 2012, available from *www.cnn. com/2012/04/11/world/africa/egypt-constitution/indexhtml.*

34. "Profile: Egypt's Vice President Mahmoud Mekki," BBC New Middle East, August 21, 2012, available from *www.bbc.co.uk/ news/world-middle-east-19255836.*

35. "Egypt: Defense chief vows to uproot militants," *Washington Post*, August 21, 2012.

36. Karen DeYoung, "From alarm to relief in Washington," *Washington Post*, August 14, 2012.

37. Barbara Starr, "Panetta tries to help secure Sinai with intel aid," CNN, August 20, 2012, available from *security.blogs.cnn. com/2012/08/20/panetta-tries-to-help-secure-sinai-wth-intel-aid/.*

38. See, for example, the analysis by commentator Fareed Zakaria on Pakistan's military posture, available from *edition.cnn. com/2009/WORLD/asiapcf/05/01/zakaria.pakistan/index.hyml.*

39. "Brotherhood leader: Morsi's Iran visit 'excellent step' if completed," *Al-Masry Al-Yom*, August 20, 2012.

40. Simon Tisdall, "Egypt underlines Iran's isolation at Non-Aligned Movement Summit," *The Guardian*, August 30, 2012. See also, "Morsi criticises Syria at Tehran meeting," *Al Jazeera*, August 30, 2012. For an interesting analysis of the Non-Aligned Movement meeting in Tehran, see Walter Pincus, "U.N.'s Ban, Egypt's Morsi deliver strong messages in Iran," *Washington Post*, September 4, 2012.

41. See "Egypt's Morsi meets Hamas chief," AFP, July 19, 2012.

42. "Gaza truce off to a shaky start," CNN US, June 23, 2012, available from *www.cnn.com/2012/06/23/world/meast/israel-gaza-violence/index.html?iref=allsearch*.

43. Isabel Kershner, "Egypt's president sends letter to Israel's, then it's denied," *International Herald Tribune*, August 1, 2012.

44. Katie Kiraly, "In their own words: Egyptian Presidential Candidates Morsi and Shafiq," available from *www.washingtoninstitute.org/policy-analysis/view/morsi-and-shafiq-the-candidates-in-their-own-words*.

45. "Israel - Officials: Sinai tanks violate 1979 treaty," *Washington Post*, August 22, 2012.

46. Jodi Rudoren, "Developments in Iran and Sinai Deepen Israel's Worries About Egypt," *New York Times*, August 22, 2012.

47. Farnaz Fassihi and Joshua Mitnick, "Mubarak Struggles as Middleman in Gaza Cease-Fire Effort," *The Wall Street Journal*, January 13, 2009.

48. Aftandilian, pp. 21-30.

49. "For Saudi Arabia, better a secular Egyptian president than a religious one," *The Times of Israel*, June 17, 2012.

50. Michele Dunne, "Managing the relationship with Egypt," *Washington Post*, July 2, 2012.

51. Phil Stewart, "U.S. military chief argues against Egypt aid cut-off," *Reuters*, February 16, 2012.

52. POMED, pp. 13-14.

53. *Ibid.*, pp. 10-12.

54. Bahraini protestors, for example, used the Pearl Roundabout in the capital city of Manama as their Tahrir Square, staging demonstrations against the government until the crackdown by the security forces.

55. Egypt did, however, participate in a regional security exercise in Jordan in May 2012. See Walter Pincus, "Middle East build up refutes Obama's critics," *Washington Post*, August 14, 2012.

56. Aftandilian, pp. 28-30.

57. See the article by Zeinab El Gundy, "Egypt activists hail Morsi's swipe at Assad at NAM summit," *Ahram Online*, August 30, 2012, available from *english.ahram.org.eg/News ContentPrint/1/0/51680/Egypt/0/Egypt-activists-hail-Morsis-swipe-at-Assad-at-NAM-.aspx*.

58. In the 1990s, for example, former Egyptian Foreign Minister Amre Moussa frequently raised the issue of Israel's nuclear weapons when commenting about making the Middle East free of weapons of mass destruction. Such speeches, which were designed to turn the spotlight on Israel, rather than Iran, were popular with the Egyptian people. At the Non-Aligned Movement meeting in Tehran in late August 2012, Morsi reiterated Egypt's stance of seeking a nuclear-free Middle East and criticized Israel for not acknowledging its nuclear weapons and not being a signatory to the Nuclear Non-Proliferation Treaty (NPT). In the same speech, Morsi said Iran had a right to peaceful use of atomic energy but said it should abide by the NPT's "international obligations," implying making all of its facilities open to IAEA inspections. See Pincus, "U.N.'s Ban, Egypt's Morsi deliver strong messages in Iran."

59. Egypt took part in a regional military exercise in Jordan in May 2012. See Walter Pincus, "Middle East build up refutes Obama's critics," *Washington Post*, August 14, 2012.

60. Available from *security.blogs.cnn.com/2012/08/20/panetta-tries-to-help-secure-sinai-wth-intel-aid/*.

61. Liberals in Egypt already believe there is a U.S.-Brotherhood conspiracy in place. See Shadi Hamid, "It Ain't Just a River in Egypt," *Foreign Policy*, July 30, 2012, available from *www.foreignpolicy.com/articles/2012/07/30/it_ain_t_just_a_river_in_egypt*.

www.ingramcontent.com/pod-product-compliance
Lightning Source LLC
Chambersburg PA
CBHW080616290526
45790CB00007B/2804